The Seven Deadly Sins Of Christian Fundraising

R. Scott Rodin

Kingdom Life Publishing
Spokane, Washington

The Seven Deadly Sins of Christian Fundraising

First Edition

Kingdom Life Publishing
P.O. Box 389
Colbert, WA 99005

To contact the author, write to:
R. Scott Rodin
21816 N. Buckeye Lake Lane
Colbert, WA 99005
U.S.A.

ISBN 0-9754399-4-4

Printed in the United States of America
10 9 8 7 6 5 4 3 2 1

Table of Contents

Introduction

Since 2002, I have been presenting a seminar at conferences and retreats entitled, 'The Seven Deadly Sins of Christian Fundraising'. The topic was developed from my theological work in the area of stewardship in general and, more specifically, from my book, *Stewards in the Kingdom*, published by InterVarsity Press in 2000. I have presented this work in Canada and the U.S. and the response prompted me to develop the seminar into this book.

When I present this topic I ask the participants to guess what these seven deadly sins might be. Over the years I have kept a sample list of what people say. The list includes: asking for too much money, poor follow-up, going on a visit without being prepared, bad research, not knowing your donors well enough, inaccurate data, not having a good volunteer base, and having an unsupportive board. Can you relate to any of these? What about the lack of a clear case, not being able to put a compelling vision in front of people, asking too often and offending your donors?

Actually all of these are right. They are all deadly to the success of our profession. But the difference is, they would be deadly sins in any arena where fundraising takes place. It is my opinion that God-pleasing development work carries with it a unique series of challenges.

Specifically, this book addresses the pitfalls of *Christian* fundraising, or better, of *Christian development work*. The questions we want to address are unique to our vocation, because our vocation is unique in the work of the Kingdom of God. They include,

- How is our work different from that of our secular colleagues?
- What specifically is so unique about Christian development work?
- What impact do these qualities have on the way we do our work?

I believe there are three things we must do to set the stage for this discussion.

First we need to define stewardship. We need to establish a biblically-informed definition of what it means to be a steward in the Kingdom of God. We cannot talk about being Christian fund raisers until we agree on what stewardship means. This is not a simple task, certainly not as simple as it sounds. It requires us to think theologically about stewardship if we are to be accurate and biblical in discerning this fundamental definition that undergirds our daily work. Therefore, we must establish a theologically-informed understanding of the biblical paradigm of the godly steward.

Secondly, we must seek to understand the spiritual battle that rages in the life of the steward. We must understand the forces that are at work in the hearts of our supporters – and our own hearts – if we are to be faithful ministers in this holy calling of development work for the kingdom of God.

And, thirdly, we will use the context of these first two views to explore what we propose as the Seven Deadly Sins of Christian Fundraising.

PART ONE
The Godly Steward

The Image of our Creator

I want you to think theologically with me for a few moments. We need to become theologians and put some of our biblical knowledge and our Christian faith to work. I want us to define stewardship by going back and thinking about God's intention for His beloved creation. We begin by reaffirming a central tenet of the Christian faith, namely, that we are created in the image of the God we know in Jesus Christ. That may be the most profound statement that human ears have ever heard. We could write volumes unpacking that statement, but here I just want you to appreciate it for a moment.

Certainty

God's self-revelation to us in Jesus Christ is the core of our faith, giving it direction and substance. How does it do this? To begin with, our faith tells us that we know our God with *certainty*. Do you believe that? While the world is searching for meaning and for some sense of who God is and how we are suppose to connect to God, Christianity proclaims that we know who our God is, *with certainty*. Jesus Christ came to us and said, "Here I am. I am the heart of God." (Colossians 1:15-20) "I am the face of God. Do you want to know who God is? Look at me." (John 14:6-7) "Do you want to know what's in God's heart? Listen to my words." (John 17:6-10) "Do you want to know what God asks of you? Follow me." (John 12:25-26).

What a marvelous and incredible truth! We know who our God is, and we know it with certainty! One reason this is so critical for us is that the Bible says we've been created in the image of God. We are created to reflect God's image in our world by what we say and do. Imagine how absurd it would be to try to reflect the image of a God who chose never to reveal him/her/its self to us in any reliable way. God would be a deceiver if he called us to reflect his image as our primary purpose in life but remained so hidden that we were constantly thrown back upon ourselves to figure out what that image really looked like. It is only by knowing God in Jesus Christ that we can embrace our call to reflect the image of God. It is a clear and joyous, albeit difficult calling.

Trinity

We also know that the God that has been revealed to us in Jesus Christ is a Triune God. Think about that for a moment. We were created to bear the image of a God who is, in his very nature, community, fellowship and interdependence.

What if this were not the case? Imagine instead that we were created in the image of a God who revealed himself as a single, un-moved, solitary distant monad out there somewhere in the universe. How would we respond if that was the image in which we were created? We'd likely be highly individualistic. We'd focus our efforts on being self-actualized. It would all be left up to us to find meaning and purpose in life. Our focus in life would be *our* future, *our* well-being because after all, we were created in the image of this very individualistic, detached God. Does this sound like some people you know? Does it sound like our national *credo* and our society's values? How many people in our neighborhoods, our work places and, dare we say it, in our churches live by the motto, 'it's all about me'?

Let's consider another popular misconception. What if we were created in the image of a deistic God, one who created us and started all the processes of our world in motion and then left the premises? This deistic God says to us, "I gave you reasoning, I gave you good minds and an abundant earth. Now it is up to you to go figure it out." To be created in the image of a deistic God would also throw us back upon ourselves to make of life all that we can. We would detach our work in science, art, mathematics, economics and other fields from our creator God. We would look to ourselves and our own achievements and happiness as the chief end and goal of our existence. God would have no bearing on our daily lives. To bear God's image in this scenario would be all but impossible. Instead we would elevate our humanity to the center of our world and 'worship the creature instead of the Creator.' (Romans 1:25)

What is most troubling about both of these views is the inevitable conclusion that we have been created in the image of a God that we can't ever really know. And that is a most absurd thing to believe! For if we have been created in the image of a God that we can never really know then we are plunged into self-delusion and despair. This view renders meaningless the teaching of having been created in God's image at all. Yet so many in our world live empty lives because they do not know the God in whose image they have been created. They have lost the central purpose of their lives by losing sight of the one who created them for only one purpose, to have fellowship with their Creator. Let us thank our gracious God every day that in Jesus Christ we know the heart, the nature and the love of our God who is for us!

For our purposes, we must consider carefully what it means for us that God has been revealed to us as Triune. This is basic Christianity, yet it is so often missed when we consider our created nature. You and I were created for relationship. That defines what it means to be created in the image of God. It is only as Father, Son and Holy Spirit that we can know God. Our God is eternally three and eternally one. And this God created us in his own image that we might bear God's image as we live in relationship.

This seems quite straightforward, yet I have had countless people say to me that in all their years as Christians they had never thought about the fact that they were created in the image of a Triune God. How about you?

This one central teaching dictates the way you and I are supposed to live. It shapes our priorities in life and brings to the center the role of relationships and community. Our identity as children of the Triune God lies in our lives lived in and through community in holistic relationship, mutually interdependent and seeking the unity of the Spirit.

That's what it means to reflect God's image. That's how we incarnate the image of a Trinitarian God. In doing so our life glorifies God, and that is precisely why we were created.

Created for Fellowship

If we look at the first three chapters of Genesis we'll find that we were created for whole relationships that reflect the image of our triune God on four levels. First, we were created for holistic relationship *with God.* Adam and Eve walked with God in the cool of the evening. Wouldn't that be wonderful? Just to hang out with God, face to face? That's the original purpose for which we were created.

Secondly, we were created for holistic relationship *with our self.* That is the relationship that is usually overlooked. We were created to have an absolute certainty of who we are, why we are here, and what we are to do. Adam and Eve didn't need to search for an understanding of the purpose and meaning in life. They knew why they were there. They were certain why they were created. Their self worth was dictated by their relationship with God. This self understanding was a part of the beautiful, holistic relationship that God wanted for all of us when he created humanity in his image.

Thirdly, we were created for a relationship *with our neighbor*; to love our neighbor as we love ourselves. That means seeing our neighbor and his/her wellbeing in the same way we see our own. It means sacrificing for the needs of others. It means valuing relationships as ends and not means to something else (something that benefits us). It means seeing our neighbor as God sees them and responding accordingly.

Fourthly, we were created for a relationship *with creation.* God put us in a beautiful garden and commanded us to take care of it and tend it. God tells us to have dominion, rule over and subdue the earth. Think about that for a moment. How do you define "have dominion, rule over, and subdue"? If you're Adam and Eve you only have one possible context in which to define these new terms. Your only point of reference is God. So, Adam and Eve were instructed to have dominion over, rule, and subdue the earth *just as God had dominion, ruled over, and subdued them.* That's what it meant to live in harmony with creation, to love it, to tend it, to take care of it.

As Adam and Eve lived out those four levels of relationship they reflected the image of God, and so do we. But unfortunately the story does not end there.

All is Lost

We know that when sin entered into the world it had a devastating impact on our relationship with God. However, too often we have limited the effects of the fall as if they applied only to our relationship to God. Here we must be sure to be true to our commitment to think theologically and holistically.

It is true, in the first case, that in the fall of Adam and Eve into sin we lost our relationship with God. Sin caused separation from God that could only be overcome through the blood of Christ. Sin banished the first couple from the garden and created a deep chasm between God and his beloved creation.

The God who was their companion became the holy and terrible God. The God who was accessible for a quiet walk in the garden was now only approachable through ritual sacrifice, human mediation and a constant need for a repentant heart seeking after unmerited forgiveness. We must not miss the radical change in this first and most important relationship due to the sin of the first human. However, we must also not stop there.

We also experienced a loss of relationship with ourselves. Adam and Eve lost their whole purpose of life. In an instant they went from walking with God in the evening and caretaking and tending his garden to dealing with God as a feared stranger who banished them out the only safe place they have ever known. The result was that Adam and Eve lost that sense of why they were, their sense of meaning. They had their primary purpose and vocation in life – fellowshipping with God and tending to his creation – thrown into disarray.

From this moment on the central theme of the history of humanity became our search to get back what was lost, to find God again and be at peace with our Creator. We are all on a search to figure out why we are here, and to recapture the intimacy with God that was lost in the fall.

On the third level we saw the rise of enmity with our neighbor. Adam blamed Eve, Eve blamed the serpent and the first story that comes after the fall is Cain's killing of Abel. Thus begins the dark history of 'man's inhumanity to man'. This inhumanity is a product of the de-throning of God and the coronation of the Self as the primary driving force in our lives. This replacement of God with Self is the core definition of the impact of sin in our lives. With self-interest at the helm, our neighbor becomes a means to our own self-promotion and a role player in our desire to increase our place and stature in his world.

We learn early in life that if people are manipulated in the right ways, they can be used to get us the things we think we really want in life. So we no longer love our neighbor as ourselves, but we *use* our neighbors *for* ourselves. Think about how difficult it is to be in a relationship where your own wellbeing is not somehow wrapped up in your relational behavior and motive. That is the pervasive presence of sin at this third level.

Finally, in this original sin we see the rise of our conflict with creation. I wonder how long it took Adam and Eve to figure out that things had changed dramatically once they were out of the Garden of Eden? It probably didn't take long. Their rule had changed from benign caretakers to toilers, hunters and defenders. Like the first couple, our relationship with creation has also been dramatically altered.

It is after the fall and through sinful eyes that we begin to change the meaning of our definitions. In a world that now looks to serve humanity and not God, "dominion" becomes *domination*, "rule over" becomes *own and control*, and "subdue" becomes *exploit.* It is a post-fall understanding of these words that have yielded the grossly mistaken assumption that the earth is ours to use any way we want. The same is true with our view of ownership. It is impossible to imagine Adam and Eve claiming ownership of part of the garden. There were no fences in Eden. No deeds, no claims, no locks and no U-Store-It buildings. After Eden, although the command to be caretakers remained in place, the idea of absolute ownership emerged and with it the entire relationship between humanity and God's creation was altered forever.

We must understand the devastating affects of sin on all four levels if we are to embrace a holistic, Biblically sound definition of stewardship, and the role of Christian fundraising that results.

All Things Restored

Praise be to God the story doesn't end there. The gracious restoration that Christ came to accomplish through his own blood was even more holistic than the affect of the fall. Paul tells us that although one sin brought this all into the world, *how much more* the blood of Christ covers all sin. (Romans 5:9-15) He also proclaims that, "As in Adam all men died, even so in Christ have all been made alive." (1 Corinthians 15:22) And we are assured that while sin brought condemnation on the one man, so the blood of Christ brings redemption for all humanity (Romans 5:12-15). In short, all that was lost in the fall was *fully and completely* restored in Christ!

A holistic understanding of what Christ did for us tells us that this restoration occurred for us on all four levels. First that our relationship with God was re-established. Through the blood of Christ we have been reconciled to God. The writer of the book of Hebrews rejoices with us that this newly restored relationship with God in Jesus Christ means that we now "come with confidence before the throne of grace." (Hebrews 4:16)

On the second level, Christ came to reclaim for us a holistic understanding of who we are as his children. In Christ we are now kingdom people. We are the people of his Kingdom; we are children of the King. As his beloved children, we have a vocation, we have a future, we have a role, we know why we are here, we know our purpose in life, and we know where we are going. That's what it means to be a Christian. All that was lost in the fall has been fully and completely restored to us in Christ.

On the third level, we have also been reconciled with our neighbor. With the Great Commission, the Great Commandment now calls us back to love one another and to take care of our neighbor. We've been called to the ministry of reconciliation, peacemaking and servanthood. We are able to love our neighbor properly because we can now love ourselves as God's beloved – and redeemed – creation.

With God's rule restored in our lives, our relationship with our neighbor can once again reflect the image of our Triune God. So we love our neighbor, care for our neighbor, serve our neighbor and enjoy fellowship with our neighbor all for God's sake and without our own agendas. That is what has been restored for us in Jesus Christ on this third level.

Finally, we have a redeemed relationship with our creation. We see ourselves once again as both the 'crown of creation' and also one *with* creation. We are given back again our true calling to care for and rule over the world with a loving and godly rule. This impacts our use of time, talents and treasures and it calls us into a true stewardship relationship with our environment.

Sadly, as Evangelicals we haven't done a very good job of seeing our redemption in Christ in this holistic way. We seem to be comfortable talking about our redeemed relationship with God and with our neighbor. Often we are not too sure what to do with our self. And we don't talk much at all about our restored relationship to creation. Yet all of this was lost and all of this was restored in Christ. And all of this has been given back to us as a free gift of grace.

The Godly Steward

This brings us to our initial definition of stewardship:

We are stewards of our redeemed and restored relationships on all four levels.

This definition is holistic and theologically informed, and it influences the way we understand our role as godly stewards on all four levels.

According to this definition we are called first to be stewards of our relationship with God. That means that worship with fellow believers in the community of faith, faithfully reading and studying the Scriptures, personal devotions, prayer, and all that we do in nurturing and deepening our relationship with God is an act of stewardship. We must always remember that our relationship with God was lost. Christ brought it back for us and has given it to us as a gift. Isn't that the most precious gift that we have ever been given? We are now called to be stewards as we honor and care for that relationship. That is the central theme of our stewardship responsibility.

Secondly, we have been restored to a whole and peaceful relationship with ourselves. It's not enough just to know that we now have purpose and reason in our life but it is something that we need to guard and care for every day. We have an enemy who works hard to get us to think that we are either more or less than what God intends. He either wants to pump us up and develop in us spiritual pride or he wants us to think that we are so sinful and disobedient that God couldn't possibly love us or do anything with us. If the enemy can push us to either side we become ineffective for the Kingdom of God. Our job as stewards is to be caretakers of our understanding of who we are as children of the Kingdom of God. We seek to maintain that balance; precious and beloved by God and also humble, thankful and obedient to his Word. We must be stewards of our self image.

Thirdly, we have been given the task to be stewards of our relationships with our neighbor. We are called to be in caring, supportive and loving relationships with one another. That means we seek to love our neighbor as ourselves. It means we work for peace and reconciliation. It means we serve our neighbor's physical, emotional and spiritual needs as the Bible directs us. As we have stated, we are called to make sure that our relationships with one another are never a *means* but always *ends*. Relationships are not stepping stones to get us to where we want to be. We are freed from the need to use people for the purpose of improving our own situation. Relationships in the Kingdom of God are always ends in themselves. We are called to love our neighbor as ourselves – period, end of story.

Finally, our restored relationship with creation calls us be stewards of God's creation and all the material possessions that we have, placing them in the service of the One Lord of the One-Kingdom. When we talk about stewardship this is usually the first relationship that people consider. I hope by now, however, that we have a more holistic, biblical understanding of what it means to be a steward. When we take this more holistic view, we understand that worshiping is stewardship. Taking care of how we see ourselves as a child of God is stewardship. Spending time with our neighbor is stewardship. Giving our money to God's purposes is stewardship.

All these areas reflect what was created, lost, and now given back to us in our glorious call to be stewards of these wonderful gifts on all four levels.

The holistic image of the godly steward is our calling, and it can be described this way:

> ***As God's people we are called to reflect the image of our creator God through whole, redeemed relationships on all four levels, bringing glory to God and practicing in each the ongoing work of the faithful steward.***

That is our definition of stewardship!

PART TWO
The Battle for the Kingdom

It's Good to be the King

If our lives as God's stewards are lived out on all four levels then we are living as One-Kingdom people. A One-Kingdom person is someone who has submitted everything on all four levels to the full authority of the one Lord who reigns over the One Kingdom of God. It means that everything we have and everything we are has been laid at the feet of One Lord in every area of our lives. That is our calling, our vocation and our joy.

The unfortunate reality is that the majority of Christians in the world are not complete, committed, holistic, One-Kingdom people. In fact, no matter how much we want to be totally and solely committed to Jesus Christ and give everything to him, there are places in all of our lives where we are still not fully One-Kingdom people.

Why is it so difficult to live consistently as a One-Kingdom person? We must acknowledge from the start that the last thing in the world that the enemy wants is for you and me to be completely committed to Jesus Christ. Our enemy desperately wants to divert our attention, sow the seeds of discontent, confuse, deceive and twist the truth just enough so that we become comfortable with those small compromises that later will grow into major distortions. It is when we are trying to live for Christ, trying to be One-Kingdom people that the enemy comes along and, in a reenactment of the temptation in the Garden of Eden, ask us,

"Does *everything* really have to be in this One-Kingdom? I mean everything? Does God really need everything in this kingdom? Consider this. You work hard, you go the extra mile and put up with difficult people. You play by the rules and as a result you earn a good paycheck and make a good living. You *earn* this money, so you ought to have some say over how you get to spend it right? I mean it just seems fair that at least your money ought to be in your control, doesn't it? Shouldn't you have a say over what happens with your *personal* funds? You've given God everything else. God will not care if you take your money and do with it as you please. Give some of it to the church, that's OK, but the rest should be yours. Doesn't God want you to be happy? And what about your job? That's not really part of God's stuff. What you do with your job and your money – and certainly with your leisure time – is really not God's concern. He is only interested in the 'spiritual' part of your life anyway. God's knows you love him and the 'churchy' part of your life looks pretty good. So enjoy the rest, you worked hard for it, after all."

Do you hear the story line? As we listen and become intrigued, slowly we begin to take little pieces of God's gifts to us and we begin to build a second kingdom - *our* kingdom. We fit it comfortably alongside the Kingdom of God. Or at least we try.

For many of us it happened another way. We came to Jesus Christ having first built a worldly kingdom for ourselves. We had sturdy walls that protected all kinds of great stuff in our kingdom. We had time and assets in our kingdom. We had relationships in our kingdom and we had our self-image in our kingdom. And who was the king in this second kingdom? We were. And, as the world reminds us constantly, *it is good to be the king.*

We were living as kings in our own little kingdoms when

Jesus Christ came along and said "No more! I have a different way for you to live." The call to live for Christ is a call to give up *all* things in our earthly kingdom. God has asked us to lay aside those things that are not of his Kingdom. The great German theologian Dietrich Bonheoffer proclaimed it clearly, "When Christ calls a man, he bids him come and die."[1] So, if you have come to Christ, God has called you to step off the throne and come into his Kingdom; fully, completely and unequivocally!

However, if we are honest with ourselves we will acknowledge that, despite this clear and unequivocal calling, we are still two-kingdom people. We continue to divide the stuff of our life between what is wholly under God's Lordship and what we want to keep under our own control. We still want to be the king.

Let's look at this at a deeper level. Here is what I hear from many Christians when we talk about this two-kingdom temptation. In our spiritual kingdom we are happy to place things like our faith, our Bible, church worship, fellowship, good works, compassion, heaven - all these 'spiritual' things. In our secular kingdom we tend to put our career, money and portfolios, our attitudes, our self-image, our friends, our personal time, and the use of creation - you know, those things that aren't really all that 'spiritual'. So our relationship to God fits very well in our spiritual kingdom while our relationship to self, neighbor, creation seem to fit better in a more worldly kingdom.

Let's take, for example, our self-image. One way to know if your relationship to yourself is in God's kingdom or your earthly kingdom is by examining those factors that influence you most in terms of your self-image. What contributes most to your self-identity? Is it how peaceful your heart is before God at the end of day? Or is in what you own? How big your house is? How much you make? Being with the right people? Is the world dictating your self-image or is it purely between you and God? As soon your stature and reputation in the world dictates your self perception, it has crossed over and become a part of your second, earthly kingdom.

Two-Kingdom Giving

We know that on this side of heaven we will always be challenged with this two-kingdom temptation. If that is true, then we can also assume that our donors are also struggling between these two kingdoms. So what does it look like when a two-kingdom person is asked to give money to a Christian cause? What is the actual transaction that takes place with regard to giving? More to the point, when the Christian development professional asks people to give money to a ministry, what are we asking them to do in this two-kingdom mind set?

If we approach the question from this viewpoint we are left with an unsettling conclusion: **giving in a two-kingdom mindset is nothing more than a transfer of assets**. In a two-kingdom world you are asking people to move some of their money (or their time) *from* their worldly kingdom *to* their spiritual kingdom, represented by your ministry. In accounting terms, you are asking donors to debit their earthly kingdom and credit the Kingdom of God.

If we buy into this two-kingdom view, then our challenge as Christian fundraisers is to determine how we get people to decrease the size of their earthly kingdom so they can increase the size of their heavenly kingdom represented by our ministry. Now let me ask you a personal question. If you are a pastor, a fundraiser or a member of stewardship committee, do you really want to invest the next five or ten years of your life to this process? Does that sound like a great reason to get up in the morning? Does it excite you to dedicate your life to answering the question, "how are we going to get these people to make this transfer of assets?" I can tell you that it doesn't excite me in the least!

Let's assume for a moment, however, that we have no other choice but to ply our trade with this underlying assumption. How do we make it happen? Why would people make this transfer? Remember your earthly kingdom defines *who you are* in this world. The world defines you by how much you own, how big your house is, what you do for a living and how successful you've been. It evaluates you on where you go on vacation, where your kids go to school, the control you have over your time and how you spend it.

So let's put ourselves in the place of our prospective donors. Let's assume our donors think in the following way,

"I have spent my whole life building my little kingdom. Maybe it's not much but it is all I have. It defines me as being relatively successful and allows me to have control over some parts of my life. I worked hard for it, I protect it and I value it highly. Now you come along and you want me to do what? You want me to decrease the size of my earthly kingdom for something spiritual? Well, you'd better give me a darned good reason why I should do that."

So what do we do? Well, we find ways of motivating our donors to make that transfer. What might we try? We could try gratitude – "God's given you an awful lot, shouldn't you be thankful and give back something to God?" That might work. Or we may try guilt, which is the other side of the coin from gratitude. After all, if you are not giving then why shouldn't you feel guilty? Guilt has long been and continues to be used a superb motivator, if not necessarily a biblical one.

How about tax benefits? The great thing about tax benefits in this two-kingdom model is that you don't really decrease the size of your earthly kingdom because you get to write off the gift at the end of the year. It's a great deal for the two-kingdom giver because, done correctly, it can actually allow you to build both kingdoms!

Then there are always the appeals to obligation and duty, which are close cousins to guilt. And what about notoriety? Names on buildings are great motivators for many. The key here again is the double benefit. If your earthly kingdom consists of pride, self worth and fame, then a naming gift might fit in quite nicely. A wrongly motivated naming gift can allow the donor actually to increase their earthly kingdom. The 'price' they pay is a donation, but they receive a greater benefit to their prestige and reputation. Pride, like guilt, can be an effective motivator in a two-kingdom world.

For the more spiritual, there is always the biblical promise that giving in this world will ensure that there will be rewards in the after-life, 'jewels in your crown in heaven'. So again at least something is getting increased in this whole process of making this asset transfer. If we motivate giving by means of a greater reward in heaven, then we are simply spiritualizing the transfer of assets, but it is still a two-kingdom transaction.

If we are honest with ourselves, don't we all fall into this trap from time to time of seeing our work as finding clever ways to get donors to part with their money? In a very real way that is all we *can* do if we are stuck in a two-kingdom mindset. In over twenty years of talking to donors I've become convinced that in the end this is the best we can do if we allow ourselves to accept the fact that we are and always will be two-kingdom people. No matter how we slice it, if we ignore the biblical command to One-Kingdom living, then fundraising will always come down to this transfer of assets.

Accommodating the Lie

The Christian development office and the local church too often help accommodate this false two-kingdom view. We do it by allowing people to live in this two-kingdom world and never challenging it as unbiblical and soul-destroying. Even worse, we too often develop stewardship programs that operate on these same two-kingdom principals, which means we are not only passively accommodating this distorted view but we are actually supporting it. If we agree to play by the enemy's rules then we are aiding and abetting this two-kingdom illusion. If we keep the issues of money and possessions as a private matter and not a concern of the church then we are communicating to God's people that the church doesn't care about these things because "that's the stuff of your kingdom."

Imagine if your pastor made the following announcement in church next Sunday,

"I'd like to come and visit with each of you and see how you are doing in your spiritual life. I want to know if there is anything else the church can do for you. I also want to be able to discern if you have any

spiritual, two-kingdom challenges in your life, so when I come I'd like to review with you your tax return for last year. That will help me see where you are spiritually."

What would be the result in your church? Chaos, furor and a hastily called 'pastoral review committee'? This inability to discuss finances in the church illustrates the extent to which the church has given over this entire arena to the enemy.

Another way we accommodate the lie is by our lack of holistic stewardship models. One great strategy of the enemy is to keep stewardship associated only with money. By not preaching and teaching whole life stewardship we make sure that nothing changes. By running our church or our ministry in no demonstrably different ways from secular organizations, we do not bear witness to the God who has redeemed all things and called us back to himself as stewards in his kingdom. Both personally and corporately, we bear responsibility for the absence of models that stand out against a backdrop of selfishness and two-kingdom values.

In this way we further accommodate a mindset that is wholly un-Christian and ultimately destructive.

The Spiritual Battle

We as Christian fundraisers must understand that if we choose to confront two-kingdom living and call God's people back to being truly One-Kingdom people, we are entering an intense spiritual battle. Christian development work, done from a One-Kingdom perspective, is all-out spiritual warfare. And it is radical. Everything else in this book follows from this key point.

When we talk about stewardship we're talking about our

people's commitment to Jesus Christ. We are talking about whether they will worship one Lord or two lords in their life. What could be more spiritual than dealing with people at this most intimate and foundational level? We must never underestimate the size of the challenge that you and I take on every day when we get up and go to work. In Money, Sex and Power, Richard Foster tells us,

> "Jesus is making it unmistakably clear that money is not some impersonal medium of exchange. Money is not some thing that is morally neutral, a resource to be used in good or bad ways depending solely upon our attitude toward it. Mammon is a power that seeks to dominate us."[2]

Later he refers to the need of every Christian to 'dethrone money'. We are called to shout 'No!' to the god money. We are called not only to deny it any power in our lives, but we are called to do the most audacious thing imaginable; we are called and invited to give it away. Imagine treating this thing that wants to be *the* god of our lives, and to be so free from it that we can, cheerfully and without hesitation, simply give it away.

When we begin to challenge this two-kingdom view, when we rebel against the demands of the god of money and seek to get others to do the same, we are going to face formidable opposition from the enemy.

I want to be clear about something here. If you decide to do your development work for the rest of your life by willingly accommodating a two-kingdom world view, then the enemy is going to leave you alone, because you are just helping to perpetuate the sense that, in the end, God really *doesn't* own everything. But, if you are willing to try to help people recommit everything in their lives to

One-Kingdom under One Lordship, watch out! You are marching into the middle of the territory that's been given over to the enemy, and you are staking your claim and saying "No More!" You are taking up the battle cry. You are facing centuries of neglect and modern cynicism about religion and money. You are taking on a consumption mentality that is feeding this two-kingdom lifestyle. You are attempting to slay sacred cows, ask questions that make people uncomfortable and even angry, and you risk being counted among the radicals.

Most importantly, as each of us takes up this challenge, we are tackling the real issue behind the allure of money. For in the end, two-kingdom living it is not really about money, it is about power. The reason it is so important to build your own kingdom in this world is not for just what it can bring us materially, but because there is power with money. And where there is greater power, there is greater control.

When a person puts everything under the one lordship of Jesus Christ they give up control. The call to One-Kingdom living is a call to the daily exercise of dying to self and rising to righteousness, of taking up our cross and following him. It is affirming with Paul that "it is no longer I who live but Christ who lives in me." (Galatians 2:20)

Second Mountain Theology

In order to enter this battle we must seek to develop a *second mountain theology*. There were two mountaintop experiences that, like bookends, marked the beginning and end of Jesus' ministry on earth. The first one occurred immediately after the baptism of Jesus by John. Jesus went into the wilderness where he was tempted three times by Satan. If we look at the third of these temptations we will hear the enemy offering Jesus all of the nations of the world, if he would just pay homage to Satan. "All this I will give to you" Satan promises (Matthew 4:8-9). And he had the power to make such an offer for as we are told he was 'prince of this world' (John 12:31, 16:10-11). Satan looked the King of Kings and Lord of Lords in the eye and said to him, "This is all mine. I can give it to you, but I own all this. This is my domain."

The scene changes dramatically, however, after the cross and empty tomb. At the end of Matthew we find Jesus standing again on a mountain. He gathers his disciples around him and says, "All authority in heaven and on earth has been given to me. Therefore go and make disciples of all the nations baptizing them in the name of the Father, and of the Son and of the Holy Spirit and teaching them to obey everything I have commanded you. And surely I am with you always to the very end of the age." (Matthew 28:18-20)

Jesus was proclaiming that the lordship of this world had changed forever. Now in the victory of the cross, he commanded the disciples to go out into the world because it belongs to only one lord. When we go into this battle I pray that we can go with that second mountain theology. Wherever we go, in what ever situation we find ourselves, we go in the victorious name of Jesus. And by doing so, we are already victorious. This is Christ's world and in His world we battle in the name of the one who is already the Lord and Conqueror. However, in this time between his first and second coming, it is still very much a battle.

If we accept this definition of stewardship, understand the two-kingdom world in which we live and view our work as a spiritual battle under the banner of a victorious Lord, then we are ready to look at the Seven Deadly Sins of Christian Fundraising.

PART THREE
The Seven Deadly Sins

Deadly Sin Number One

Being Unprepared for the Battle

The first deadly sin of Christian fundraising is being unprepared for the battle. I want to ask you as a Christian development professional, are you spiritually ready to engage in this battle? Are you willing to walk into the enemy's territory, put your stake in the ground and say 'we are not going to do our work according to two-kingdom values'? Are you ready to engage in the hard process of calling our people back to whole, One-Kingdom living? Are you ready to challenge them to be truly godly stewards where everything is under the Lordship of God? For anyone involved in Christian fund raising work, before attaining the skills and training for *what* you do, you must first focus on *who you are.*

I believe that who you are as a child of God and where you are in your relationship with Jesus Christ is more important than all the tools you will learn in all the seminars and all the conferences that you will attend for the rest of your development life.

You can learn all the techniques and master all the tools of fund raising, but if you are not ready for the spiritual battle you will fall back into the easier course of accommodating a two-kingdom view of life. Who we are as Christian fund raisers is more important than what we do. And developing our spiritual depth and character is the most important thing we can do for our work in development.

All Christian development work depends on the strength of our relationship to Jesus Christ and our openness to the work of the Spirit.

Putting on the full armor of God is a wonderful way to go into your daily development life. Read Ephesians 6:10-18 and think about what that means in relationship to your battle right now against the enemy and the control that the enemy has in the lives of the people with which you work. Wisdom and discernment come from prayer, study, and personal devotion. Where are you? How is your prayer life? How faithful is your devotional life? These are stewardship questions, and they will determine how effective you will be as a development person in the Kingdom of God.

Daily prayers and devotions are essential and for that reason *the development department should be the most prayerful place in every ministry and Christian organization.* Did you hear that? The development department should be the most prayer-bathed place in your entire organization. Do you want to turn your ministry's understanding of fund raising around? Lift up the work of your department as ministry. Model for your organization that Christian development people are people on their knees in prayer. They are people who ask for prayer and people who view all of what they do in kingdom terms.

When I started at Eastern Seminary as vice president for advancement we decided every morning that we would start in prayer. We got our department together and spent twenty minutes of dedicated prayer time every morning. Although it was difficult with travel schedules and meeting schedules and phone calls and e-mail demands, we did it every day without fail. I found out later that we had become known as the department that faithfully prayed every morning.

Have you heard this perspective before?

"You fund raisers are the necessary evil of Christian ministry, right? You go out and do what none of the rest of us wants to do. In fact, we're not even sure what you do is really Christian work, but thank heavens you do it because you give us the money we need so we can do the *real* ministry."

Where does ministry happen in your organization? Most people would point to a variety of places where it 'happens', but few, if any, would include the development department. We can begin to turn that around and help people understand that we are co-ministers of the Gospel, that the work that we are doing with donors requires fervent and frequent prayer. Can your development department be the most prayerful place in your entire organization?

When you hire new staff I would challenge you to place the depth of their spiritual relationship with Christ as the number one characteristic you look for, because that's going to dictate their success more than any other factor. The development staff should be the most spiritually mature people in your organization. If you are on a church staff, be careful not to repeat the mistake of many churches. They elect all the deeply spiritual people as Elders, and elect the brand new Christian or a business person with a questionable level of spiritual maturity to serve as Trustee. If dealing with money is dealing with dynamite, and if we are in a spiritual battle in our work with finances, shouldn't the most godly people in the church be the Trustees?

The enemy will work in every Christian church and ministry to create a false sense of security, minimizing the battle and the need for preparation, prayer, and total reliance on God. Plan and prepare seriously for the battle. Commit never to go into this Kingdom work spiritually unprepared. Equip your people to be spiritually prepared for the battle that they will face everyday.

Deadly Sin Number Two

Self-Reliance over Spirit-Reliance

The second deadly sin comes when we place self-reliance over spirit-reliance. Let me ask you a few questions. Do you ask people to pray over their giving decisions? Do you really mean it? In the end do you hope that final decisions to give result from the donor, as a child of God, coming before the throne of God and asking what God would have them do? Do you pray that when they sense that God is laying something on their heart, that they will do it obediently, no matter what it is?

Our answers to these questions will demonstrate the level of our reliance on the Spirit in giving decisions. We all would like to say that we rely solely on the work of the Spirit to move our donors to give as God leads. But what role do we really leave for the Spirit to play? Why do we leave this to the Spirit, and when do we start to interfere with the Spirit's work? Do we ever get impatient and give in to the use of technique and pressure to 'close a gift'? Do we give in to the temptation to believe that in the end it's really up to us? Do we dwell on whether we made the best presentation, said the right words, sent the most compelling materials?

It is true that we are called to do everything we can to present professionally and clearly a credible need before a ministry partner and ask them for the right amount, for the right project, at the right time. That's our job. But then do we really step back and we leave the giving decision in the hands of God?

We struggled with this during my years at World Concern, a ministry of CRISTA Ministries in Seattle. We were gifted with an outstanding photographer who had the ability to capture the most horrific and honest moments of human suffering in a way that preserved dignity and still engendered deep compassion. His photographs were stunning, and often we were left with the decision about both the appropriateness and the necessity of using them. We needed to walk a fine line between honestly portraying the need and using graphic images of suffering as a way to move our donors to give. I hope we always erred on the side of modesty, believing that if we told the story in words and pictures in an honest but respectfully reserved way, God's people would respond through the prompting of the Holy Spirit and not because they were shocked by Jon's photographic genius.

The question we faced in the end was this: where does our reliance ultimately rest? The enemy will work constantly to develop a self-reliant mentality in our work. The end result will be that we may ask donors to pray but, in our hearts we really believe that it is up to us to close the deal and get the gift.

We also must reject falling victim to a scarcity mentality. This un-Biblical mindset believes that there are not quite enough resources to go around. It places us in competition with one another in God's kingdom. As a result, I have to be a better fund-raiser than you because I don't want you to get *my* donor. We see this when pastors refuse to give ministries access to present to their congregation for fear that their parishioners will give to outside ministries, with the result that less will be left for the church. This assumes God doesn't have enough resources to fund his work through his people. That's a scarcity mentality. We must not give in to this distortion. God is the God of abundance. And if his people will respond with obedience there's enough money to fund every need of every church and every para-church ministry pressed down, shaken together, and overflowing. There are enough funds to meet the needs of every work of God on the face of the earth. What we lack is not funds, but funders – faithful, godly, holistic, obedient, One-Kingdom stewards.

Our job as Christian development professionals is to cultivate a spirit of trust and dependence on God for all things in every aspect of our development work. And to help our own organizations do the same in every area of ministry. I know that one of the greatest sources of friction in an organization is when the need for dollars comes up against the command to trust God in all things. But we must always hold firm to the belief that if we do our work with integrity to the best of our ability, we can confidently leave the results in God's hands, the God of abundance!

The temptation will always be to grab that control back for ourselves, and when we do, we have committed the second deadly sin. When we trust in God we expect great things and we watch with anticipation for what he will do for our ministry through our faithful development work.

Deadly Sin Number Three

Money over Ministry

The third deadly sin is placing money over ministry. This is related to Deadly Sin #2, but it has something important and new to add. Despite the pressure to raise money, the spiritual growth and well-being of our ministry donors must take precedent over asking for funds. The truth is that the two often happen together. In fact we might define our development work as "enabling God's people cheerfully and joyfully to do what God puts on their hearts." Now that's ministry! God *does* love a cheerful giver. God *does* reward faithfulness in people's lives and we are in the privileged position of giving people opportunity to do that every day when we ask them for their support. We give people the opportunity to fulfill what God has called them to do - be good stewards in God's Kingdom.

Sometimes, however, the two do not happen together. You may have been on a lead gift solicitation where, just before it came time to ask for the gift that your ministry so desperately needed, you found out in conversation that something was happening in this person's life that indicated it was not the right time to put this ask on their heart Meanwhile, back at the office you have an entire development staff and a president and a capital campaign steering committee waiting to know if we are going to get that million dollar gift! Which takes precedence - care for the donor or the financial needs of the ministry into which you have been called? Have you ever been tempted to do whatever it takes to get the gift?

Deadly sin number three is committed whenever the pressure for money is lifted over care for our donors. It's a hard choice but trust, faith and relationships are the media in which we work. Genuine caring about our supporter's hearts must always have priority over the urgency of a gift. Care for your people and God will bless the rest.

I have worked with college presidents who have cultivated relationships with major supporters for years without ever believing the time was right to ask for the lead gift. I was in the same position myself as a seminary president. I spent years visiting a supporter who had significant potential for a major gift. We built a relationship and she gave some generous gifts, but never at the level of which she was capable. Despite my cultivation work, the time was never right in her life to ask for that level of gift. Two years after I left the seminary, her situation changed, and my successor made that ask and received one of the largest gifts in the seminary's history. I was tempted to think, "Why didn't I make that ask when I was there?" However, as I thought back on my visits with her I was convinced that the timing was not right, and an ask of that amount would have been inappropriate and uncaring. I rejoiced in the success of my colleague and for the work that her gift will fund for the building of the kingdom. However, I would not be honest if I did not say that I felt a twinge of the envy that comes from the enemy when he can get us to believe that we must apply the pressure necessary to get the gift, especially when we will get the credit.

The enemy will use anxiety, doubt and a false sense of urgency to shift your focus away from the ministry focus of our development work and onto the pursuit of immediate returns. Cultivate a ministry mindset in your development work and never let it be unseated as your first and highest calling.

Deadly Sin Number Four

Unwillingness to Invest the Time

Deadly sin number four is the unwillingness to invest the time required of a faithful development program. Building trust and relationships takes time. This goes back to our understanding that relationships are *ends* and not *means.* From my experience of over twenty-three years, this is one of the hardest things to commit to every day. I have to pray that God will daily remind me that the value in every relationship lies in far more than the financial support that may result. To do that, I've got to be willing to invest the time. Time to sit with partners when things are difficult, time to call our partners, time to call them again, time to be sure that our partners know that we care about them, time to thank them, time to involve them, time to give them space and time to challenge them to higher levels of commitment.

Ministry requires presence, being with people. Consider this sentence: "short cuts almost always require some level of manipulation and coercion." I wrote that a number of years ago and now in looking back at it I can affirm that it is still true. Every time you short circuit that relational process in order to get a gift, somehow you've got to introduce some sense of manipulation or coercion.

If we are in a spiritual battle we must be willing to engage for the long haul. Impatience is a deadly enemy. (If you need to go back to your president or CEO and tell them that I said that, please feel free to do so.) What I have learned in my years in this field is that impatience is always costly. So we need to be granted the time it takes to do our work in a God-pleasing way. We must ask of our leadership that we be given the time to build our department or conduct our campaign the right way.

There is perhaps no greater indicator of a total lack of understanding of our work than to believe that it can be sped up or slowed down according to the funding needs of the institution. If donors are commodities to be manipulated then this is perfectly sound reasoning. If, however, these are ministry partners, and if our work is to minister to them through our ministry as Christian development professionals, then relationships – and the time they demand – must rule the day.

The enemy will create an impatient spirit within you and tempt you to use manipulation and coercion to close the deal. The enemy will subtly shift your focus from relationships as an *end* to relationships as a *means* only. As a result we too-often use relational language as a ruse for manipulation and even exploitation.

I was with a new development officer doing training for building a major gifts program. I was talking about the importance of relationship and several times he responded with comments like, "yes, that's a great way to get your foot in the door", or "if we can get them to trust us it will be easier to get to know their net worth and ask for bigger gifts." I asked him about the value of building strong relationships and ministering to those who support us, even if it does not lead to a larger gift. His reply? "What for, that's not our job, we are here to raise money, aren't we?" Are we? This is where several of our deadly sins come together. If we rely on the Holy Spirit to move our donors to final decisions, and if we believe our work is ministry, is it really *our job* to raise money? Or is it our calling in the context of caring relationships to present to God's people credible opportunities to serve the kingdom with their time, talents and treasures?

Build the necessary time into your developmental planning to value these God-given, precious relationships, and don't deviate for the sake of expediency.

Deadly Sin Number Five

Decisions without Discernment

Deadly sin number five is the temptation to make decisions without discernment. What is your process for seeking God's wisdom in your fundraising decision? Decide with your team what your process will be for making sure that you have God's word in every decision you make. How consistent are you in seeking God's guidance in everything you do? Or put more bluntly, when do you stop seeking to hear God's voice and start asking him to bless what you were going to do anyway? Are you and your team truly committed to discerning God's will and way in everything? Once you hear God's voice will you follow it regardless of what it requires or where it leads? That is the essence of One-Kingdom living.

Consider the situation of King David as recorded in First Chronicles chapter 14. The story begins,

> *When the Philistines heard that David had been anointed king over all Israel, they went up in full force to search for him, but David heard about it and went out to meet them. Now the Phil istines had come and raided the Valley of Rephaim.*

David had a problem. The raiding Philistines were challenging his authority early in his reign. And David responded with a prayer for discernment,

> *So David inquired of God: "Shall I go and attack the Philistines? Will you hand them over to me?" The LORD answered him, "Go, I will hand them over to you." So David and his men went up to Baal Perazim, and there he defeated them. He said, "As waters break out, God has broken out against my enemies by my hand." So that place was called Baal Perazim. The Philistines had abandoned their gods there, and David gave orders to burn them in the fire.*

This was not unusual for David who most often sought the Lord in prayer. However, the story continues,

Once more the Philistines raided the valley.

Here is what I find remarkable. My tendency would have been to say, "I know what God wants me to do here. This is the same problem as we faced before. Same problem - same solution. So I don't need to ask for guidance. Surely God will want us do the same things as we did before." And off I would march…to defeat. Not David. Listen to the rest of the story,

> *So David inquired of God again, and God answered him, "Do not go straight up, but circle around them and attack them in front of the balsam trees. As soon as you hear the sound of marching in the tops of the balsam trees, move out to battle, because that will mean God has gone out in front of you to strike the Philistine army." So David did as God commanded him, and they struck down the Philistine army, all the way from Gibeon to Gezer. So David's fame spread throughout every land, and the LORD made all the nations fear him.*

David was not presumptuous, and God was again faithful. The enemy will tempt you to listen to your own voices, trust your own ideas, and short cut the discernment process. We need to go to God and listen to God and know God's heart in all we do. Here are five areas that I believe demand incredible discernment if we are to carry out our work as ministry.

The first area is in the identification of potential donors for our work. We need to bathe this process in prayer that God might open our eyes to see those whom he has brought into our sphere to help fund our work. Do we listen intently to the leading of the Spirit in identifying potential new supporters?

The second area is our work of laying the right project or

opportunity in front of our supporters. It is impossible for us to know what is on the hearts and minds of every one of our donors. When we prepare to make an ask, we need to listen to the voice of the Spirit as we discern the best project or giving opportunity to present. We want our supporters to be blessed through their generosity, and if we can match their passion with our need, then everyone is blessed

The third area is in the timing of our solicitations. We touched on this above and it should be clear how critical it is to be sensitive to discern the right time to ask and the right time to step back. For all of the research that we can do, there is no substitute for the prayerful request for God's wisdom.

Fourth, we need this divine discernment in our planning processes. I lead a lot of board strategic planning sessions and help dozens of organizations write major strategic plans. For all of the work we do on right sequencing, scenario planning, inclusive processes and 'out of the box' thinking, the greatest asset we have as Christians is the quiet moments we spend in prayer, presenting our plans to God and seeking affirmation in the community of faith.

Finally, we need this special, Spirit-filled discernment in our dealing with our colleagues. Development can be stressful work, and to do it well we must hire, train and manage our development staff effectively. Each of these processes requires clear discernment. For all of our greatest intentions and best worded goals and objectives, we must have the right people in the right places in our organizations to realize our fullest potential for the kingdom. Finding them and keeping them requires a level of wisdom and discernment that demands a committed prayer life. When the prophet Samuel anointed David as king, he was not following a recommended executive search process. He was following the leading of the Spirit of God. If it is truly God who looks at the heart, not just the outer appearance, then we need this divine wisdom in our work of hiring and keeping the best possible people to carry out God's work.

There are countless other areas where God's wisdom and Spirit-filled discernment are critical for our work. Cultivate a discernment mindset. Commit the time and hold each other accountable. That is why the people working in your developmental department have got to be spiritually mature people; people who have a passion for Christ and who want to listen for the work of the Holy Spirit in everything they do. If you assemble a team of people who have that kind of spiritual maturity, then investing in discerning prayer will be as natural as breathing. It's a blessing to the Kingdom when people who are committed to make discernment the center of what they do commit themselves to the ministry of fund raising.

Deadly Sin Number Six

Activity without Accountability

Deadly sin number six is yielding to the temptation to have activity without accountability. In this spiritual battle, accountability is critical. Here are some questions to consider. What systems do you have in place in your ministry to ensure that funds are spent according to how they were designated? Are donor calls undertaken with a clear ministry intent? Is there a clear set of guidelines and adequate training for everybody before they go on a donor visit? Is prayer a part of every donor ask, making sure that the askers' hearts are right? Are your development plans built on a solid biblical foundation with the guidance of the Spirit? Is your development staff committed to the ongoing growth of their personal walk in Christ? Does your development department get away on spiritual retreats, and is that acceptable within your organization?

Perhaps we should think about accountability as a series of audits that we voluntarily undertake on a regular basis. Here are five to consider.

Financial Audit. I am surprised at how many ministries I come across who do not have a current financial audit, and many who have *never* had one. It is a cost that simply must be invested to ensure that all financial records are in the best possible order. We are handling donor money, and that fact alone should demand that we have a regular audit. Beyond the formal audit, we must be sure that we are honest managers of our ministry money. That includes opening our books up to a scrutiny on our fund raising expenses, and spending funds only as designated, for starters. Every ministry working in the name of and for the sake of our Lord Jesus Christ must develop and maintain the highest standards of fiscal integrity. Keep your books audited and keep them open.

Time Audit. Finances are easy to audit when compared to time, but time may be more important. There are few mechanisms available to undertake a full time audit like there are for finances, but nonetheless we are called to account for our stewardship of our time. This is where our colleagues can help. Are we willing to be open to the constructive feedback we could receive if we asked our co-workers to tell us how well they believe we use our time? How about our superiors and those who report to us? Our colleagues work with us every day, and few people are better positioned to expose our time wasting habits. If you can open yourself up for honest dialogue, you will find ways to improve your use of time, and provide yourself with a built-in accountability system as well.

Attitude Audit. Like time, attitudes are hard to look at objectively, but they are major determinants to our performance. How can you check ungodly attitudes before they affect your work? First, we can hear the words of Paul who encourages us to do as he did and "take captive every thought and make it obedient to Christ." (2 Corinthians 10:5). We need to guard our minds against the divisive and soul destroying thoughts that the world continually sends our way. Thoughts, once invited into our minds on a regular basis, take root and foster attitudes that are detrimental to our walk with Christ and our work as development professionals for the Kingdom of God. Again co-workers here can also be a great source for helping us diagnose these attitudes. Give your co-workers the permission to challenge you when they sense in you an un-Christ-like attitude coming through your words or actions.

Motivation Audit. From time to time in this field we need to take an honest assessment of the motivations that drive us. It is so easy for the pressure to raise more money, the desire to be seen as successful or the temptation to steal the glory to cloud and confuse our motivations. This is a matter for prayer and frequent, deliberate attention.

Spiritual Audit. Finally, we need to have a daily discipline that ensures a healthy and robust spiritual life. This can only be realized through the development of personal devotional lives and spiritual disciplines. This dimension is crucial to the effectiveness and faithfulness of the Christian fund raiser. Make it your highest priority and do not let the pressures of the day or the drive for results rob you of a rich, disciplined inner spiritual life with God.

The enemy will seek to drive wedges of secrecy and sow self-deception into your development work wherever there is a lack of accountability. The result will be bad attitudes that harden and once-clear motivations that get cloudy. The enemy will seek to deceive you into allowing the creep of financial expediency to create compromise in your accounting. He will seek to rob you of your time and sow in you a spirit of resentment against those who are best positioned to help you through accountability.

We cannot underestimate the importance of accountability nor deny that this is a major area of battle with the enemy. Victory here is vital! Dedicate yourself to developing a clear accountability system in your development program at every level and give it the authority it needs to be a true corrective.

Deadly Sin Number Seven

Stealing the Glory

Finally, the seventh deadly sin is stealing the glory. How do we balance acknowledging donors, rewarding successful fundraising work, and giving God the glory for all good things? We have to do all three and do them well. It is important that we acknowledge and thank our donors properly. We must also acknowledge the work of the development staff and our volunteers. But we must do these things in the full recognition that God gets the glory in all we do.

We acknowledge donors appropriately when we understand that they are simply being obedient to what God has laid on their hearts. I want to pause here and remind us of what we have said previously. People who are stuck in a two-kingdom mindset and who see giving as the decrease in value of their earthly kingdom in order to gain some benefit in their spiritual kingdom will expect to be acknowledged in a different way. They may expect a letter from the president, a parking space outside the new gym or their name on a plaque.

One-Kingdom people don't care about such things. I have over-thanked a One-Kingdom person and been rebuked for it. What a wonderful and refreshing thing it is to have somebody say, "why would you invite me to a special dinner to thank me for doing what God asked me to do?" or "why would you put a plaque on the wall with my name just because I was being obedient?" That's One-Kingdom thinking. Hopefully through our work we can encourage more people to be One-Kingdom people. We still need to thank our supporters, but it's a whole different process when you are dealing with One-Kingdom people. Thank God for them.

We also need to recognize our development staff and volunteers appropriately. We must be sure that everyone in our organization understands the role of the people in development as true ministry and not as some detached 'sales force'. We need to find creative ways to acknowledge and thank the work of our development staff that focuses on their entire ministry achievement and not just the financial bottom line.

Finally, and most importantly, we must glorify God as the true source of all funds and every blessing. We must glorify God for the ministry accomplishments as much as the fund raising accomplishments. Imagine if at the end of a successful capital campaign the program booklet you put out had two thermometers. One showed how the campaign met its goal and raised so many millions of dollars. Praise be to God. The other one showed how, in the course of running this campaign, X number of our supporters acknowledged that they became more committed in their walk with Jesus Christ. Wow! And, all because of a fund raising campaign!

Run your development campaigns with the goal that every donor becomes closer to Jesus Christ because of the way we are raising this money. Make it your highest goal that every supporter is impacted by the gospel because of the way you are presenting your case and what we are modeling in the way you conduct your work. Give God the glory not only for the money raised but for the lives that have been touched for Christ in the process.

The enemy will work to divert any and all glory away from God. This is the enemy's number one job in all the world. He will take any glory he can get and divert it away from God.

He will put it on anybody and anything else he can. Don't let him! Have a plan for appropriate donor acknowledgement, and for staff and volunteer recognition. But glorify God above all else!

The Christian Development Office

Fund raising is a growing field of professional calling and vocation. It has standards, credentials and offers a strong career path. There are hundreds of books and seminars and conferences and workshops that teach how to do it from every conceivable angle. It is part of the fiber of our country from our tax codes to our philanthropic ethos. With fund raising such a prevalent part of our culture, and its practice so well-honed across the spectrum of not-for-profit agencies, our work must stand out as uniquely *Christian* development work.

How is that lived out in your work every day? I believe that this is *the* question facing us as Christian fundraisers! Everything else we discuss and plan and teach is ultimately and invariably tied to how we answer this question. I have tried to develop an argument that these seven areas belong uniquely to the work of Christian fund raisers who understand the call from our Creator God to be holistic stewards on all four levels. This does not mean that we might not share some techniques and practices with our secular colleagues. It does mean that we measure our work according to a different set of standards and we understand that our obstacles and barriers come from a different source. As such, we face unique challenges that stem from our base motivation for our work, namely, to glorify God and build His kingdom. From this perspective come the seven deadly sins, and our attention to them is critical if we are to be effective as uniquely *Christian* fund raisers.

My heart goes out to every development person who seeks to honor God in all she or he strives to do. You are on the front lines. You face a colossal battle with eternal consequences. So here is my charge and prayer.

1. **Plan and prepare seriously for the battle and commit never to go into this without being spiritually prepared.**
2. **Cultivate a spirit of trust and dependence on God for all things.**
3. **Cultivate a ministry mind set in your development work and never let it be unseated as your first and highest calling.**
4. **Build the necessary time in your development planning and do not deviate for the sake of expediency.**
5. **Cultivate a discernment mind set; commit the time and make it a priority.**
6. **Develop a clear accountability system throughout your development program and give it authority.**
7. **Have a plan for appropriate donor acknowledgement and staff recognition, celebrate your victories and glorify God above all else.**

I will close by sharing with you my favorite fund raising story from Scripture. I do not think it is often viewed as a story about faithful asking and generous giving. The story comes from Luke, Chapter 19 beginning at the 28th verse.

"And after Jesus had said this he went on ahead going up to Jerusalem. As he approached Bethphage and Bethany at the hill called the Mount of Olives he sent two disciples saying to them, "Go to the village ahead of you and as you enter it you will find a colt tied there which no one has ever ridden. Untie it and bring it here. If anyone asks you why are you untying it? Tell them, "The Lord needs it." Those who were sent ahead found it just as he had told them and as they were untying the colt its owner asked them. "Why are you untying the colt?" They replied, "The Lord needs it."

Jesus sends his disciples ahead of him, telling them they are going to find a colt tied up in front of a certain person's house. They are to go up, untie the colt and bring it to Jesus. He also tells them that if anybody comes out and asks them what they are doing they are to say, "the Lord needs it." Armed with this directive they go into Jerusalem.

We know from the history of that time that a colt was a very prized possession, one of the most valued possessions a household could own. It would one day serve as transportation, pull a plow, cultivate fields and carry items to market. In short, this young colt was going to play a major role in the health and prosperity of this family.

So these disciples come along and find the colt as Jesus had said and, as they were instructed, they start untying it and leading it away in broad daylight. The Scripture says that the owner sees all of this happening and his response is a simple question, "why are you untying that colt?" That may be what he said, but I don't think that is how he said it. I think he likely picked up a stick and began running out at them yelling in anger at the top of his lungs, "*why are you untying that colt?!#%&!?*"

All that the disciples say in response to the man's protest is what Jesus had instructed them to say, "the Lord needs it." The Lord needs it. We assume that the owner of the colt knew who "the Lord" was and that the Lord was his Lord, too. And that is all that the owner needed to hear. What a response of faith!

The owner of that precious colt did not need a direct mail fundraising letter. The disciples did not take out a brochure and say, "well, this colt is part of the Triumphal Entry Campaign. As you'll see here by our table of gifts we need five contributions at the 'colt level' and we are hoping you would consider giving one of those today." They offered no plaque on the walls of Jerusalem. No seat next to Jesus at the major donor banquet.

"The Lord needs it." That is all the disciples said to this angry man brandishing a stick. And upon hearing those words, the man just let it go. What a marvelous picture of a heart tuned to God. ***Imagine what it must have been like for that man in a few short hours to see the King of Kings and the Lord of Lords riding triumphantly into Jerusalem on his own colt.***

I love this simple example of a One-Kingdom person giving sacrificially for the right reason and then seeing what amazing things God does with that gift. My prayer is that in working with our donors we can help them become generous givers by cultivating an obedient heart. As we do, our life's work becomes the joyous task of telling God's people about great opportunities to invest in the work of the kingdom. We ask them to search their heart and ask themselves if God is saying to them, "I need you to share what I have given you that this work may be completed." And we pray and trust that they will respond obediently, which, in Kingdom terms, always means abundantly and joyfully.

A Prayer for my Colleagues

Gracious Lord, I thank you for every person reading these words and for the ministries that they represent. I thank you for the work that they do. I thank you for their hearts. I thank you that they've given their life to you and seek to live out their vocation in this very important ministry. I pray for each of their ministries. I pray for every campaign that is going on right now. I pray for every donor right now who is considering an important gift to the ministries represented by these readers. I pray for every battle that is being fought in development departments internally. I pray for every staff opening that needs to be filled with a man or woman of God. I pray for every ounce of doubt that's in my reader's minds about what the future might hold for them and their work. Lord, minister to every heart that reads these words. Call us completely and wholly to you. Equip us every day to do this incredible work you have laid upon our hearts. And prepare us to be astonished by your abundance as you work in our ministry and our lives that you may receive the glory, in Jesus' name. Amen.

---

1 Bonhoeffer, Dietrich. *The Cost of Discipleship*. New York: McMillan, 1948, p. 73.
2 Foster, Richard. *Money, Sex and Power.* San Francisco: Harper and Row, 1985, pp. 25-26.

About the Author

R. Scott Rodin has been in Christian not-for-profit leadership for over twenty-two years. He is currently the president of Rodin Consulting, Inc.

Dr. Rodin has held consulting and development posts with firms including The Frank Group, World Concern, University Preparatory Academy, the University of Aberdeen, Scotland, and Eastern Baptist Theological Seminary. He has served as fundraising counsel to over one hundred organizations in the United States and Great Britain including Christian colleges, seminaries, schools, churches and para-church ministries in the areas of leadership, fund raising, strategic planning and board development.

From 1997 to 2002, Dr. Rodin served as the President of Eastern Baptist Theological Seminary in Philadelphia where he also taught theology and ethics.

Dr. Rodin holds a Master of Theology degree and a Doctor of Philosophy degree in Systematic Theology from the University of Aberdeen, Scotland. He is a nationally-sought speaker and preacher. His books include, *Abundant Life,* (Steward Publishing, 2005), *Stewards in the Kingdom,* (InterVarsity Press, 2000), and *Evil and Theodicy in the Theology of Karl Barth,* (Peter Lang, 1995).

Dr. Rodin is married to Linda, and they have three children, Anthony, Ryan and Lindsay. Dr. Rodin resides in Spokane, Washington, and he can be contacted at rodinconsulting@aol.com.